JUNIOR
BIOGRAPHIES

W9-BTL-349

Kathy Furgang

RUTH BADER
GINSBURG
SUPREME COURT JUSTICE

Enslow Publishing
101 W. 23rd Street
Suite 240
New York, NY 10011
USA

enslow.com

SHOREWOOD-TROY LIBRARY
650 DEERWOOD DRIVE
SHOREWOOD, IL 60404

appeal To ask a court of law to reverse a decision.

discrimination Unfair treatment based on sex, race, age, or another category or difference from a group.

dissent Disagreement with a majority opinion.

gender equality Fair treatment no matter a person's sex.

judge A person who makes decisions about legal cases.

lawyer A person who argues legal cases and defends someone in a dispute about the law.

majority More than half of a group.

nominate To formally suggest.

Senate Part of the United States Congress involved in making laws and policies.

CONTENTS

Ruth Bader Ginsburg

In 1933, the United States was a very different place than it is today. Back then, it was very rare for a woman to become a lawyer. It was even more unusual for a woman to be a judge. One child born in that era, however, challenged those ideas when she grew up.

Joan Ruth Bader was born on March 15, 1933, in Brooklyn, New York. The family lived in a low-income section of that part of New York City. Ruth's father, Nathan, had come to the United States from Russia. Her mother, Celia, was born in New York to Austrian parents. Ruth's father was a merchant, and her mother worked at a clothing factory.

As a young girl, Ruth's family called her "Kiki," a nickname started by her sister.

Ruth grew up in the Flatbush area of Brooklyn, New York, in the 1930s and 1940s.

GROWING UP

At the time Ruth was growing up, not many girls went to college. Many women got married and raised children at home. They never had a career. Ruth's mother encouraged her to study hard and go to college.

Ruth Bader Ginsburg Says:

"My mother told me to be a lady. And for her, that meant be your own person, be independent."

Ruth followed her mother's advice. Sadly though, Celia Ginsburg was not able to see the results of her daughter's hard work. She died of cancer the day before Ruth's high school graduation. Ruth went on to attend Cornell University. She finished first in her class.

Chapter 2
Practicing the Law

The year 1954 was important for Ruth in more than one way. Not only did she graduate from college, but she got married, too. Her husband, Martin Ginsburg, was a law student at Harvard University at the time. He was called into the military when they were expecting their first child, Jane.

When Marty returned from the military, the young family moved near Harvard University so he could continue law school. That's when Ruth decided that she would also like to become a lawyer. She enrolled in Harvard Law School. She was just one of nine women in the class of more than five hundred students.

Ruth and Martin Ginsburg, seen here in 1998, met on a blind date.

Ginsburg's husband suffered from cancer when the couple was first married. She cared for him and their young daughter while she attended law school.

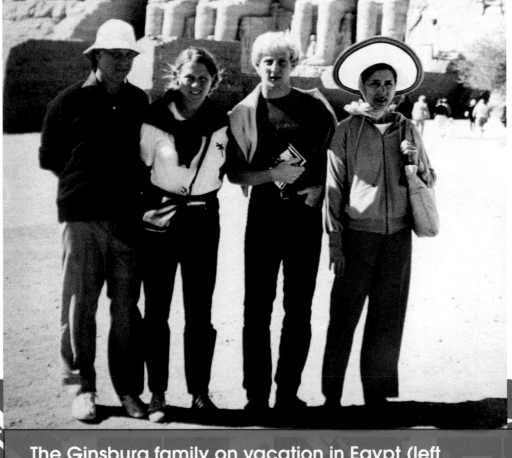

The Ginsburg family on vacation in Egypt (left to right: Martin, Jane, James, and Ruth)

FIGHTING FOR EQUALITY

The Ginsburg family moved to New York City when Marty got a job there as a lawyer. Ruth finished law school in the city, at Columbia University. She had a much harder time finding a job than her husband did. At the time, there were few law firms that wanted to hire a woman.

Ruth Bader Ginsburg Says:

"When I graduated from Columbia Law School in 1959, not a law firm in the entire city of New York would employ me."

The experience made an important impression on Ginsburg. When she was finally hired, she decided that a lawyer could help change unequal treatment based on gender. She took cases that could help others who were not treated fairly under the law.

Ginsburg in 1963. As a young lawyer, she saw that she could make a difference by taking on discrimination cases.

ARGUING HER CASE

Ginsburg's first gender inequality case involved a woman in the military. The woman was not given the same benefits as men in her same position. Ginsburg lost the case. She realized that it would be difficult to convince men of the court that inequality toward women was unfair. So, for her next gender inequality case, she defended a man who was treated unfairly because of his sex. She won that case. This put her in a better position to argue that men and women should be treated equally.

Ginsburg defended many different people. Each one was treated unfairly in different ways: in the military, with insurance, with education, and with pregnancy in the workplace. Ginsburg became known for the cases she won. The results of the cases changed people's lives. Over time, discrimination based on sex became less acceptable. Companies knew they could not get away with unfair treatment.

Ginsburg continued to argue legal cases. At the same time, she taught law at universities and wrote books about law. The 1960s and 1970s were important years for cases about discrimination. More women were starting careers. More minorities were becoming successful in business. Ginsburg became known as a successful lawyer who won important cases about discrimination.

Ginsburg in 1977. At this time, she was a law professor at Columbia University.

Ruth Bader Ginsburg Says:

"I try to teach through my opinions, through my speeches, how wrong it is to judge people on the basis of what they look like, color of their skin, whether they're men or women."

In 1980, President Jimmy Carter noticed Ginsburg's work. He **nominated** her to an important position as a court judge. She was nominated to serve on the United States Court of Appeals for the District of Columbia Circuit. The **Senate** voted and approved her to that position. She and the other judges reviewed all **appeals** of government cases in Washington, DC. It is considered one of the most important positions for a judge in the country.

Ginsburg is sworn in as a Supreme Court justice in 1993, with President Clinton (*left*) and her husband beside her.

> The position of Supreme Court justice is for life, or until the justice chooses to retire.

THE HIGHEST COURT

Ginsburg spent thirteen years on the appeals court. Then she was chosen for the highest honor in law. In 1993, President Bill Clinton nominated Ginsburg for a seat on the Supreme Court. To be a justice on the Supreme Court, a person is first nominated by a president. Then the Senate votes about whether the person should have the position. The vote was 96 to 3 in favor of Ginsburg.

Ginsburg has been on the Supreme Court for decades. She is known for having an opinion different from many of the other judges. When justices disagree with the **majority** of the

court, it is called a **dissent**. Ginsburg has dissented on many cases. She makes her opinion known in careful statements that explain her point of view. The dissents help to show how she interprets the law. They also help form public opinion about important issues.

Ginsburg is known for the lace collars she wears with her robe.

Ginsburg is one of only four women who have served on the Supreme Court. Sandra Day O'Connor served from 1981 to 2006. Sonia Sotomayor has served since 2009. Elena Kagan has served since 2010.

Ginsburg poses with the other female Supreme Court justices: Sonia Sotomayor (*left*) and Elena Kagan.

Ruth Bader Ginsburg Says:

"Fight for the things that you care about, but do it in a way that will lead others to join you."

Ginsburg has become popular with young people who admire her views on fairness and equality. Her nickname is "Notorious RBG," after a popular rapper.

Shaping the Future

Ginsburg's husband, Marty, died of cancer in 2010. After decades on the Supreme Court, Ginsburg is more popular than ever. She speaks at public events, and she is known for her love of opera and traveling.

The Supreme Court affects the way Americans live. They make decisions about issues like same-sex marriage, equal pay, women's health, and the rights of people with disabilities. The court will continue to interpret laws and help protect people's rights under those laws. As a member of Supreme Court, Ginsburg has stayed true to herself as she works for fairness and justice.

TIMELINE

1933 Ruth Bader is born on March 15, in Brooklyn, New York.

1950 Ruth's mother, Celia, dies on June 25, a day before Ruth's high school graduation.

1954 Graduates from Cornell University and marries Martin ("Marty") Ginsburg.

1955 Daughter Jane is born.

1959 Graduates from Columbia Law School.

1965 Son James is born.

1980 Nominated by President Jimmy Carter to the US Court of Appeals for the District of Columbia Circuit. Approved by the Senate.

1993 Nominated by President Bill Clinton to be a Supreme Court justice and approved by the Senate.

2010 Husband, Marty, dies of cancer.

BOOKS

Carmon, Irin, and Shana Knizhnik. *Notorious RBG: The Life and Times of Ruth Bader Ginsburg* (Young Reader's Edition). New York, NY: HarperCollins, 2017.

Halligan, Katherine. *Herstory: 50 Women and Girls Who Shook Up the World.* New York, NY: Simon & Schuster, 2018.

Levy, Debbie. *I Dissent: Ruth Bader Ginsburg Makes Her Mark.* New York, NY: Simon & Schuster, 2016.

Winter, Jonah. *Ruth Bader Ginsburg: The Case of R.B.G. vs. Inequality.* New York, NY: Harry N. Abrams, 2017.

WEBSITES

Congress for Kids

www.congressforkids.net

Check out this site for kids interested in learning about how the government works, including the judicial branch, which includes the work of judges throughout the country.

Government and Constitution

www.government-and-constitution.org/united-states-government/judiciary-branch.htm

Learn about the role of the judiciary branch in the United States government, including the role of the Supreme Court.

History.com: Ruth Bader Ginsburg

www.history.com/topics/womens-history/ruth-bader-ginsburg

Visit a website that has a full biography of Ruth Bader Ginsburg.

Index

Published in 2020 by Enslow Publishing, LLC.
101 W. 23rd Street, Suite 240, New York, NY 10011

Copyright © 2020 by Enslow Publishing, LLC.

All rights reserved.

No part of this book may be reproduced by any means without the written permission of the publisher.

Library of Congress Cataloging-in-Publication Data
Names: Furgang, Kathy, author.
Title: Ruth Bader Ginsburg : Supreme Court justice / Kathy Furgang.
Description: New York : Enslow Publishing, 2020. | Series: Junior biographies
 | Includes bibliographical references and index.
Identifiers: LCCN 2018047858| ISBN 9781978507906 (library bound) | ISBN
 9781978508835 (pbk.) | ISBN 9781978508842 (6 pack)
Subjects: LCSH: Ginsburg, Ruth Bader–Juvenile literature. | United States.
 Supreme Court–Officials and employees–Biography–Juvenile literature. | Women judges–United States–Biography–Juvenile
 literature. Judges–United States–Biography–Juvenile literature.
Classification: LCC KF8745.G56 F87 2019 | DDC 347.73/2634 [B] –dc23
LC record available at https://lccn.loc.gov/2018047858

Printed in the United States of America

To Our Readers: We have done our best to make sure all website addresses in this book were active and appropriate when we went to press. However, the author and the publisher have no control over and assume no liability for the material available on those websites or on any websites they may link to. Any comments or suggestions can be sent by e-mail to customerservice@enslow.com.

Photos Credits: Cover, p. 1 MCT/Tribune News Service/Getty Images; p. 4 Alex Wong/Getty Images; pp. 6, 14 Bettmann/Getty Images; p. 9 The Washington Post/Getty Images; pp. 10, 19 © AP Images; p. 12 Walter Oleksy/Alamy Stock Photo; p. 16 Jeffrey Markowitz/Sygma/Getty Images; p. 18 Mark Wilson/Getty Images; p. 20 Barbara Alper/Archive Photos/Getty Images; interior page bottoms (scales of justice) blankstock/Shutterstock.com.